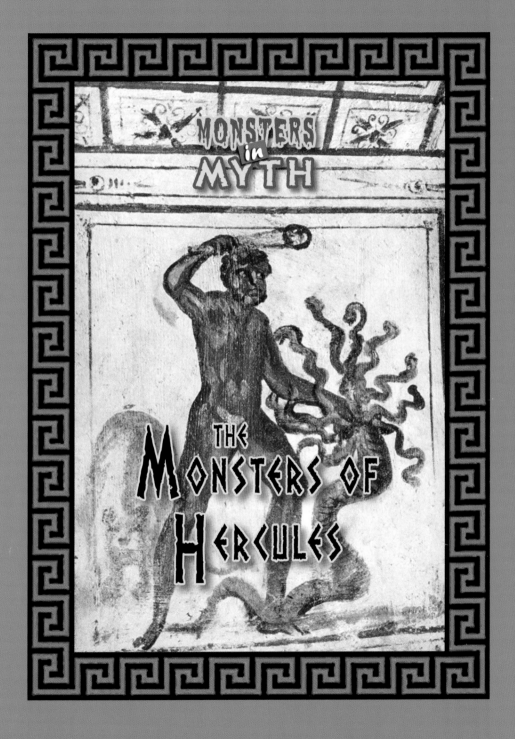

MONSTERS in MYTH

THE MONSTERS OF HERCULES

MONSTERS in MYTH

TITLES IN THE SERIES

Monsters *in* MYTH

THE MONSTERS OF HERCULES

Tamra Orr

Mitchell Lane
PUBLISHERS
P.O. BOX 196
HOCKESSIN, DELAWARE 19707
VISIT US ON THE WEB: WWW.MITCHELLLANE.COM
COMMENTS? EMAIL US: MITCHELLLANE@MITCHELLLANE.COM

Mitchell Lane
PUBLISHERS

Printing   1   2   3   4   5   6   7   8   9

Library of Congress Cataloging-in-Publication Data
Orr, Tamra.
  The monsters of Hercules / by Tamra Orr.
      p. cm. — (Monsters in myth)
  Includes bibliographical references and index.
  ISBN 978-1-58415-927-8 (library bound)
  1. Heracles (Greek mythology)—Juvenile literature. 2. Hercules (Roman mythology)—Juvenile literature. I. Title.
  BL820.H5O77 2011
  398.20938'01—dc22
                                                                    2010028764

ABOUT THE AUTHOR: Tamra Orr is the author of more than 250 books for readers of all ages. In addition to covering Hercules and his Labors, she has also written *The Sirens, Achilles,* and *Apollo* for Mitchell Lane Publishers. She lives in Portland, Oregon, with her family. In her free time, she enjoys reading, writing letters, and hanging out with her teenaged children.

AUTHOR'S NOTE: In this book, the Roman version of the hero's name, Hercules, has been used. It is the one by which most Americans know him. To the Greeks, he was known as Heracles (HAYR-uh-kleez). Other characters and places in this story are given their Greek names. The legend of Hercules has many variations. This version follows the most commonly told versions. Though based on the myths, dialogue and specific events in this book are imagined—just as the dialogue and events in myths are imagined.

PUBLISHER'S NOTE: This story is based on the author's extensive research, which she believes to be accurate. Documentation of such research is contained on page 46.

The internet sites referenced herein were active as of the publication date. Due to the fleeting nature of some web sites, we cannot guarantee they will all be active when you are reading this book.

To reflect current usage, we have chosen to use the secular era designations BCE ("before the common era") and CE ("of the common era") instead of the traditional designations BC ("before Christ") and AD (*anno Domini,* "in the year of the Lord").

TABLE OF CONTENTS

MONSTERS OF HERCULES

Hercules is always portrayed as a handsome hero, complete with curly hair and a noble face—and usually wearing the hide of a lion. At New York City's Metropolitan Museum, this statue honors the hero's looks as well as his bravery.

MONSTERS OF HERCULES

CHAPTER 1

A Moment of Madness

When Hercules (HER-kyoo-leez) opened his eyes and looked around him, he could not believe what he was seeing. The sight of the brutal slayings was so painful, he feared it might blind him. He knew that he certainly would never be able to forget the sight and suspected he would not even be able to live with the knowledge of it. He thought about screaming or crying. He considered begging the gods to end his life immediately. Hercules was frightened that any second he would go mad. Then he realized that madness was exactly what had caused this horror in the first place.

A Hero in the Making

For most of his life, Hercules, or as the Greeks knew him, Heracles (HAYR-uh-kleez), had had a golden life. As the child of the mortal woman Alcmene (alk-MAY-nee) and Zeus (ZOOS), the most powerful god of all, Hercules had amazing powers from the very beginning. As a baby, he had proven to everyone that he was something special when serpents crawled into his crib. Instead of screaming in terror like his twin brother Iphikles (IH-fih-kleez), he strangled both of the serpents before they could sink their fangs into either of the boys. He would not discover until years later that Hera (HAYR-uh), the wife of Zeus, had sent the snakes to kill him.

Hercules strangling the serpents

When the snakes failed to kill the infant Hercules, Hera knew that she had to make new plans. She wanted to do everything she possibly could to make this young boy's life miserable. Why? She wanted revenge! When Alcmene named the baby Heracles—meaning "Hera's glorious gift"—that just made the goddess angrier. She vowed that she would make the baby boy pay for his mother's attitude. She would just have to wait until the perfect moment—and it was coming.

Growing up, Hercules became handsome, with golden curls, rippling muscles, and godlike abilities. Some of the most well-known and respected teachers spent time showing him the skills Greek young men were expected to know. He was shown how to drive a chariot, how to wrestle an enemy, and how to shoot a bow and arrow. He was trained in the art of war. He was even taught how to play a lyre—the only skill he could not quite master.

By the time he was eighteen years old, Hercules had managed to outfit himself with some of the most awesome weaponry in the world. From Apollo (uh-PAH-loh), the god of light and music, he had a bow and arrow. Hermes (HER-meez), the messenger god, had given him a sword; and Hephaestus (heh-FES-tus), god of the forge, had created a special golden breastplate for him. His horses had come from Poseidon (poh-SY-dun), god of the sea; and his robe from Athena (uh-THEE-nuh), goddess of war and wisdom. He had even fashioned himself a powerful club. He was ready to go out into the world and conquer whatever enemy got in his way. Fate—or Hera—had other plans for him, however.

Hercules' skill with a bow and arrow would save his life—and end the lives of many monsters.

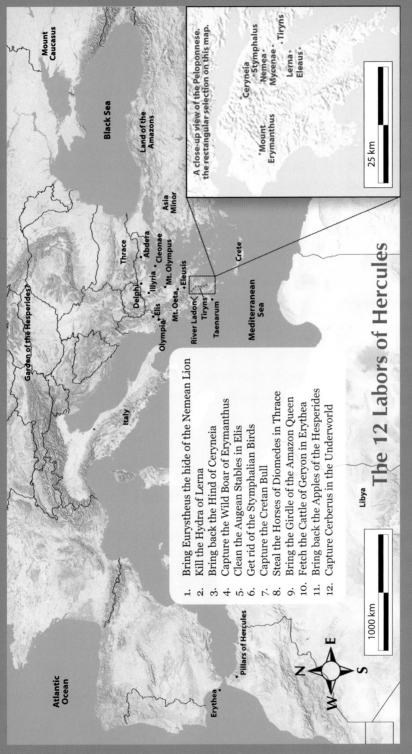

The 12 Labors of Hercules

1. Bring Eurystheus the hide of the Nemean Lion
2. Kill the Hydra of Lerna
3. Bring back the Hind of Ceryneia
4. Capture the Wild Boar of Erymanthus
5. Clean the Augean Stables in Elis
6. Get rid of the Stymphalian Birds
7. Capture the Cretan Bull
8. Steal the Horses of Diomedes in Thrace
9. Bring the Girdle of the Amazon Queen
10. Fetch the Cattle of Geryon in Erythea
11. Bring back the Apples of the Hesperides
12. Capture Cerberus in the Underworld

A close-up view of the Peloponnese. The first few labors were accomplished on the rectangular selection on this map.

25 km

1000 km

Hercules' travels took him all over Greece and beyond the Mediterranean Sea. The first few labors were accomplished on the Peloponnese, but as the labors grew harder, they were also farther from Tiryns.

Marriage, Family, and Disaster

Hercules spent his time battling for good and helping people wherever he went. When he did a favor for a man named Kreon (KREE-on), the grateful leader gave Hercules his daughter Megara (mee-GAYR-uh) in appreciation. The two were married and quite happy. As the years passed, they had several children. All of that came to a crashing end when Hera decided that her perfect moment had finally arrived.

Hera cast a spell onto Hercules that threw him into a blinding rage. Without being aware of what he was doing, he killed Megara and their children. When he woke up from the spell and realized what a horrible thing he had done, he felt he could not possibly live another day. He decided that he should exile himself—just remove himself from the rest of the world so that he could pay for the sin of what he had done. Before doing so, though, he went to see the Oracle at Delphi to ask for some guidance. There he was told that, even though he had not meant to commit the act, he must cleanse the evil from his spirit.

How was he to do this? The Oracle told him to go to Eurystheus (yoo-RIS-thee-us), the King of Tiryns and Mycenae (my-SEE-nee). He should serve this man—known for being cruel and for being a coward—for a dozen years and, over that time, perform twelve tasks for him. Each mission was dangerous and close to impossible. Most of them involved facing ferocious beasts and ravenous monsters. If Hercules survived the assignment, his prize would be not only a clean soul but immortality. If he did not survive—he refused to think about that possibility. It would take all of his courage, his strength, and his patience to endure the twelve labors. As Hercules said in Homer's *The Odyssey*: "I was a son of Zeus, but infinite was my suffering; for I was slave to a far inferior man, and heavy were the labours he laid upon me."[1]

A Regretful Boast

Alcmene, the mother of Hercules, was tricked by Zeus. He pretended to be her husband, who had been gone a long time. Just before she gave birth to her twin boys, Zeus bragged that a boy was about to be born who would grow up to be a mighty ruler. Hera overheard him and knew that he meant Alcmene's baby, so she started making a sneaky plan. First, she went to Zeus and made him promise that the next baby boy born would be a leader. Then, she went to the gods that controlled childbirth. She had Hercules' birth delayed and the birth of another boy—Eurystheus—sped up. Next, she went to Zeus and told him what had happened:

Zeus and Hera

> "Today is born an illustrious man who will rule
> Over all the Argives: Eurystheus, son of Sthenelos,
> Descended from Perseus, sole born of your own stock.
> He is not unfit to rule over all the Archives."
> So she spoke, and a bitter sorrow struck Zeus
> Deep in his heart. . . . and ever afterwards
> He would grieve when he saw his own dear son
> Toiling at one of his shameful tasks for Eurystheus.[2]

Instead of Hercules getting the position of ruler, it was given to Eurystheus, the very same man who would one day demand that Hercules perform a dozen desperately difficult missions for him.

The Nemean lion had been terrorizing the countryside for years. Eurystheus was sure it would devour Hercules as easily as it had preyed upon countless others.

MONSTERS OF HERCULES

CHAPTER 2

A Powerful Mane, an Immortal Head

I could hear someone slowly, carefully, making his way through the forest, stopping to listen every few steps. I crept closer, keeping my belly to the ground. This man wasn't like the others who had come for me before. He did not look frightened. He was not breathing fast or sweating. Instead, he looked calm and determined. I preferred my hunters shaking.

I am the son of Typhon (TY-fon), a fire-breathing giant with 100 snake-heads on his shoulders and serpents for legs, and Echidna (eh-KID-nah), beautiful woman on top, serpent below. What a home life I had. My brothers are Orthus, a two-headed watchdog; and Cerberus (KER-ber-us, or SER-ber-us), the many-headed hound who guards the gates of hell. My most annoying sibling is the Sphinx. Having a sister who looks like a woman, a lion, and a bird is confusing enough, but she was always telling me riddles that I simply could not figure out. Thankfully, she took up guard duty at the gates of Thebes, where she devours people who can't answer her riddles.

For countless years, I've been roaming the foothills of Nemea, hunting for prey—animal or human. Farmers have tried to stop me, of course. Brave men occasionally gather and make plans, come up with new strategies to slay me before I can carry off any more villagers or livestock. Grabbing whatever weapons they can find, from sharp rocks to bows and arrows to little more than a heartfelt prayer to Zeus to protect them, these men creep up the hillsides to hunt me down.

Careful as these men are, I can always hear them coming. Their voices carry on the breeze, along with that delicious scent of human flesh. It makes my stomach rumble every time. Their clanking weapons and sneaky movements always announce their approach. Quietly, I stay hidden in the tall grass, my tawny fur blending in to make me practically invisible. I like

to toy with them, letting them get close, and then BOOM! I leap out and attack.

I am unstoppable. Weapons do not slow me down. Arrows cannot pierce my skin. Neither can the sharpest knives or pitchforks. A strike from a club might make me pause—if anyone should ever get close enough to use one. With my sharp claws and even sharper teeth, few have gotten that far. Those who manage to escape only run back to the villages to warn others to stay away. I rule the land.

Now there is a new stranger approaching. When he is just five feet away, I let out a mighty roar that echoes all around us. Instead of running away, he's standing up to face me! I burst out of the trees, teeth bared, heading directly for the hero-like man. He grabs his bow and arrow and sends off a frantic shot. The arrow bounces off my glorious hide, and my chest swells with pride. The man shoots again. Once again, the arrow falls to the ground. Can he see me smiling? I let out another low growl and prepare to swipe him with my terrible claws.

A club swings around and smites me in the head, stunning me for just a moment— long enough for the man to wrap his powerful arms around my neck and squeeze hard. I can smell his sweet breath as he grunts and increases his grip, more powerful than I have ever felt before. Then I can smell nothing, for my breath is gone.

Hercules chokes the life out of the powerful lion.

Taking His Prize

As the lion's body sagged into his arms, Hercules was grateful for his wrestling lessons. His first assignment was over. He had heard the lion's hide was impenetrable, but couldn't believe it when his weapons glanced off without even scratching the beast. When he tried to skin the lion, as Eurystheus had insisted he do, he found that his knives would not cut the hide, either. Then he had another idea. He used the lion's own sharp claws, and they worked perfectly. When he was finished removing the lion's skin, he wore it as a helmet and cloak. It would help him with his future labors.

A Cloak of Honor

In his play *Heracles*, Greek playwright Euripides (yoo-RIH-pih-deez) wrote, "First he cleared the grove of Zeus of a lion, and put its skin upon his back, hiding his yellow hair in its fearful tawny gaping jaws."[1] Many paintings, sculptures, and other works of art portray him with this fur cloak around his shoulders. Wearing it, he returned to give the lion skin to Eurystheus as he was assigned. The king was so frightened when he heard of Hercules' strength, he would not allow the hero past the city gates. Instead, he ordered his smiths to make a large bronze jar. He hid inside it until Hercules left again on the next mission.

Many urns and other pieces of art show the battles that Hercules fought—and won. The Greeks began making these vases in the seventh century BCE. The art form, which showcased their mythology, reached its peak in the sixth and fifth centuries BCE.

Facing the Hydra

It is fantastic being the Lernean Hydra, one of the fiercest monsters in the world. Like the Nemean lion, I am the offspring of Typhon and Echidna. We have an odd family, but since I have nine glorious heads, I am always the one who gets the last word. I also have an important secret—one of my heads is immortal. My home is in the wonderfully wet and smelly swamps of Lerna. I come out only long enough to terrorize the people and grab a tasty human snack whenever the mood strikes me.

But, what is this? A young hero approaches and he is not alone. Another young man is by his side. Both look brave, the fools. It will take more than two to defeat me, of course.

They are shooting flaming arrows outside my den. Why? When I crane one of my serpent heads around to peek outside, the tall man chops it off!

The many heads of the Hydra are also often shown on pieces of art. Sometimes she is portrayed as beautiful—others times more like a serpent. No matter how she looked, she was always dangerous.

In this 1875 painting by Gustave Moreau, Hercules faces the Hydra, armed with little more than his courage and a club.

That hurts! But no matter—two more are already growing back in its place.

Seeing the look of shock on his face is worth the agony of his sword. Now I am more powerful and beautiful than I was before. I let out a fierce hissing roar, and one of my many servants, the giant crab, joins me in the battle. It immediately bites at the men's ankles and feet. They begin to retreat!

Now they are back, with the older man brandishing his sword and his helper swinging a torch. Every time the man cuts off one of my heads, this irritating boy burns the stump so that nothing can grow back. What trickery! I can't get away!

In a tile painting at the University of Gothenburg, Sweden, Hercules and his nephew Iolaus are surrounded by the poisonous heads of the monster.

But I will still win because of my immortal head. When they chop that off, too, I shriek—and then everything goes quiet and black.

The End of Hydra

Hercules was grateful he had brought Iolaus (EYE-oh-lus), the son of his twin brother, to face the Hydra. They had to work together to destroy the many-headed beast. After they had cut off the last head, they buried it under a rock. Hercules also took a moment to dip his arrows in the monster's poisonous blood. He would find good—and not so good—uses for those arrows in the years ahead.

From Myth to Entertainment

The many adventures of Hercules, along with those of his nephew Iolaus and others, have been translated into countless movies, television shows, and even cartoons. In 1997, Disney produced a full-length animated movie called *Hercules* that starred the voices of Rip Torn and Tate Donovan. It was then turned into a regular television cartoon show from 1998 through 1999. *Hercules: The Legendary Journey* was a television series that ran for six seasons, from 1995 to 2001. It starred actors Kevin Sorbo as Hercules and Michael Hurst as Iolaus. A number of other films have been made over the last few decades with Hercules at the center of the story. Arnold Schwarzenegger portrayed the hero in the modern remake *Hercules in New York*. Another bodybuilding actor, Lou Ferrigno, of *The Incredible Hulk* fame, played the role in *Hercules* and *Hercules II*. The hero even appeared in *The Three Stooges Meet Hercules* in 1962.

In addition, stories about Hercules and his missions have been written in a number of books, graphic novels, and comic books. The twelve labors of Hercules have also been used as part of the plot of other novels, such as Agatha Christie's *The Labors of Hercules* and Andy McDermott's *The Tomb of Hercules*. Marvel Comics has produced a line of comic books about the hero, and he often shows up in comic books featuring Thor. He has been honored with action figures and trading cards. Even the composer Handel wrote an entire symphony to honor Hercules and his bravery.

Hercules kept winning his battles—and Eurystheus kept hiding from him in his urn.

MONSTERS OF HERCULES

CHAPTER 3

From a Boar to the Birds

I lift my hairy snout into the breeze and catch the flowery scent of a human. I can hear him as he draws close to my den, for he's shouting at the top of his lungs, calling, "Come out, you foul boar!" When the golden-haired young man appears, I begin snorting and trampling the dirt. I want him to know exactly where I am before I attack.

Normally my home in northwest Arcadia is peaceful—for me. The nearby villagers do not think so, of course, because I love to come out of my lair on Mount Erymanthus every day and search for something fun to chase—and delicious to eat. Beware anyone or anything that comes too close, for goring my prey with my sharp tusks is my favorite way to snag a meal. I have lost count of how many brave men tried to stop me, only to see nothing but a blur as I stuck my tusks in and tossed them in the air. Sometimes I catch them. Sometimes I let them splatter on the ground. I always hear them creeping up the mountainside, whispering and planning how they will catch me. But it's no use. They are no match for me.

Before I can gore the blond-haired man, he begins chasing me around the mountain. This man has much more energy than the others. I keep running—but so does he, and I tire before he does. I need to rest, and I need water. Doesn't he need to catch his breath, too? I dash into some thick bushes to rest for just a moment.

Ouch! A spear has struck me through the branches. I back up more and more and then fall into some deep snow. The cold feels great and will rejuvenate me. I close my eyes for just one moment. . . .

Suddenly, a net settles down around me. The man gathers it up, with me inside, tosses me over his shoulder, and begins walking. "This will please King Eurystheus," he mutters as he goes.

Miles later, I hear the man ask for the king. He is hiding in his jar, so he doesn't even get to see me. What a coward!

Adventures Along the Way

Between taking care of the Hydra and subduing the Erymanthian boar, Hercules had gone on an adventure that did not involve a wicked monster. He had to catch a golden hind, a small deer, and bring it back to the king. Since the animal was sacred to the goddess Artemis, capturing it would risk her anger. This mission took more than a year to accomplish.

Before he reached the lair of the boar, he had yet another adventure. He stopped on his travels to spend some time with a friend. Pholus (FOH-lus) was a centaur, a creature that is horse from the waist down and man from the waist up.

This Roman mosaic, made up of thousands of tiny tiles, dates from around 118 to 138 CE. While centaurs valued family, most of them were not civilized. They fought using rocks, and they became violent when they drank wine.

The majority of these animals are wild, violent, and scary. Pholus, on the other hand, was friendly and had good manners despite living in a cave. He invited Hercules in to have dinner with him. When Hercules asked for some wine, however, Pholus hesitated. The wine belonged not just to him but to all of the centaurs. When Hercules opened the bottle, the aroma of the wine drifted through the forest and the other centaurs smelled it. They were angry! Galloping to the cave, they tried to attack Hercules with rocks and branches, but he fought them off with the arrows he had tipped with the Hydra's poison. He managed to scare off or kill a number of the centaurs. When Pholus picked up one of the arrows his guest had used, a drop of the poison landed on him and he died as well. Hercules paused, filled with regret, and took the time to bury his friend.

Terror from Above

Have you heard the stories about man-eating birds with nasty claws and beaks made of bronze? You know, the rumors about the Stymphalian (stim-FAL-ee-un) birds being pets of Ares (AYR-eez), the god of war? They are all true—I should know. I am one of them. I and my flock are vicious birds that enjoy nothing better than to dive-bomb the humans below and steal a lock of hair—or an ear or a nose. From high up in the trees, we silently watch and listen for the approach of another animal or, even better, some foolish man who thinks he can escape from us. As soon as the creature comes close enough, we rise as one and soar down through the leaves and branches, our shiny metal beaks and fierce claws ready to rip it apart.

How could anyone possibly get rid of all of us? It is not possible. Some fools have tried, of course, and sometimes we have lost one or two from our flock, but we are too mighty together to be beaten.

We are circling a man now, screeching as loudly as possible to either drive him away or drive him crazy, whichever comes first. What can this young hero do?

Hercules would battle with another centaur much later in life. As the centaur lay dying, Nessus tricked Hercules' seond wife, Deianeira, by telling her his blood was a love potion. Instead, it was poison.

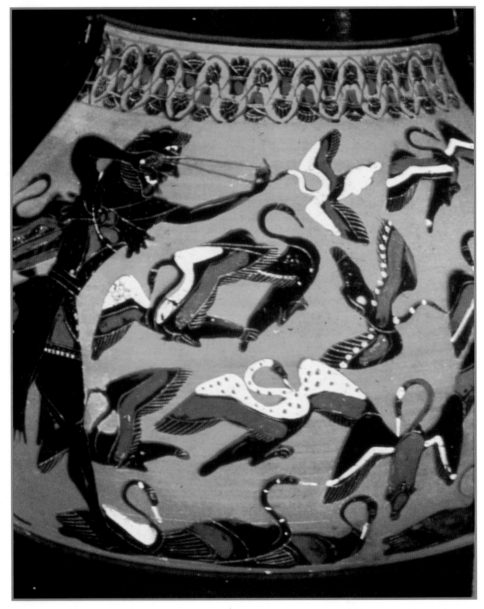

The birds surrounded the hero, doing all they could to make him leave, but they were no match for his patience and his aim.

As we prepare to dive upon our victim, a horrible rattling sound, like metal banging and pinging, makes us fly straight up into the air. The man begins pelting us with stinging shot. Is he using a slingshot or a catapult or bows and arrows? Members of my flock fall to the ground like rain. When I am hit, I know our kind is doomed.

Another Mission Off the List

Before he scattered the birds, Hercules had to accomplish his fifth mission. This one had not been dangerous or bound to irritate a god. Instead, he had been assigned to clear out the Augean stables—no easy job, as it held hundreds of horses. Hercules, however, merely diverted a river and washed away the filth.

Many of the myths about Hercules explained odd land formations or natural phenomena such as volcanic eruptions. In Liguria, rocks litter the ground. One myth says they fell from the sky when Zeus was helping Hercules fight an army of thieves.

When he was finished with that, it was time for the sixth mission. He was to get rid of huge flocks of birds that were deep in the woods surrounding Lake Stymphalus in northeastern Arcadia. For this labor, he had the help of the goddess Athena, who gave him a set of metal castanets to flush them out of the forest. They were made by Hephaestus, the god of the forge.

Some versions of this story make this mission look like one of the easiest. How difficult could it be to scare off a bunch of birds? However, other versions describe the adventure as being just as challenging as the others. Pausanias, a second-century writer, described the birds in *Description of Greece*:

> These fly against those who come to hunt them, wounding and killing them with their beaks. All armor of bronze or iron that men wear is pierced by the birds; but if they weave a garment of thick cork, the beaks of the Stymphalian birds are caught in the cork garment. . . . These birds are of the size of a crane, and are like the ibis, but their beaks are more powerful, and not crooked like that of the ibis.[1]

Whether these birds were fierce, man-eating creatures or just a flock of irritating birds, the mission was accomplished—the birds were on the ground. Hercules was ready to move on to the next challenge.

The God of Fire

Some stories say the god of fire and metalworking—often referred to as the divine blacksmith—was the son of Zeus, and some say he had no father at all but was simply the son of Hera.

When Hephaestus was born, Hera saw that he was lame and, embarrassed at this physical flaw, she tossed him out of Olympus. Lucky for him, he landed in the great river of Ocean which flowed around the world. Nymphs—female creatures of the sea—saved him and kept him in a cave by the ocean for nine years. It was there that he learned all the skills of blacksmithing, using his metalworking skills to make jewelry for the women who took care of him. Once he had become quite talented at metalwork, he got revenge on his coldhearted mother by sending her a golden throne that trapped her the minute she sat down in it.

Years later, he forgave Hera—and even defended her against Zeus, who was furious at the way she had treated Hercules. This time, Zeus threw Hephaestus out of Olympus, and he landed on a faraway island of Lesbos. The blacksmith went on to build everything from golden and bronze palaces for the gods to beautiful arms and armors for gods and mortals.

The powerful god of metalworking spent endless hours hammering and shaping pieces of gold, copper, silver, and bronze.

Homer wrote about his ability to control fire in *The Iliad,* when Hephaestus boils away the water in the river Xanthos:

> The river blazed with fire, his lovely stream seething,
> And as a cauldron boils, set on a fierce flame,
> melting the fat of a well-fed hog, bubbling up
> on every side as dry sticks burn beneath,
> so Xanthos' lovely streams were burned with fire,
> and the water boiled, and would not flow along,
> but was stripped by the mighty blast of Hephaestus.[2]

The fabulous bull of Poseidon was meant to be a sacrifice to the sea god. When it was allowed to live, it became a killer.

MONSTERS OF HERCULES

CHAPTER 4

Capturing a Bull, Catching the Herd

Yes, I'm a grazer—but I feed on humans and other cattle (even though I'm a bull). I used to live on Crete, where Poseidon, the god of the sea, sent me as a gift to King Minos. The king had promised Poseidon that he would sacrifice me in the god's honor—but the moment he saw me, he knew that he would not be able to do it. What a relief! It is true that I am extremely rare and beautiful! Luckily, King Minos sacrificed a different bull in my place, hoping that that one would be good enough to please Poseidon. It was not. The god was upset by the broken promise. He swore to find a way to get revenge on King Minos.

The god of the sea put a spell on the king's wife, Pasiphae (PAS-ih-fay), so that she would fall madly in love with me. I have to admit—I am handsome and the plan worked. Together, she and I had a son and we named him Asterius (as-TEE-ree-us). As he was half man and half bull, he came to be known as the Minotaur, which means "the bull of Minos." Poseidon also made me savage.

One day, I was minding my own business when a young muscle-bound man approached me. Without any warning, he reached out and grabbed me around the neck. I had never felt anything so strong. He held on no matter what I did. I bucked and kicked. I stood up on my hind legs and shook. It did not matter. He would not let go. Finally, I gave in. I had no air left and could not fight any longer. At last he relaxed, and reluctantly, I allowed him to ride on my back across the sea to Mycenae. Once King Eurystheus saw me, he had no idea what to do with me. In the end, Hercules set me free, and I made a new home in Marathon—where, of course, I went right back to hunting down cattle and terrorizing their owners. After all, that is what I was made to do!

Man-Eating Horses

We are so excited, for another visitor has just arrived. I am one of the four wild, uncontrollable, and, we must admit, incredibly beautiful mares of Diomedes (dy-AH-muh-deez), son of Ares and King of the Bistones (bis-TOH-neez) in Thrace. Diomedes keeps us chained up with iron in bronze mangers at all times. He cannot trust us to get loose because, for as long as we can remember, he has been feeding us with human flesh. When he invites visitors and guests over for dinner and they accept, they don't realize that they are going to be the main course. It's not our fault that he's been feeding us his victims for years, but now we have a terrible desire to

The mares of Diomedes had a hunger for human flesh that seemed unending. Only Hercules knew the cure they needed.

kill and eat any human that comes too close. And now the man and his traveling companion, Abderus, have entered the stable.

Why are they fighting with our grooms? We whinny as we watch each of our handlers fall to the floor of the barn. The stranger unchains us and we try to nip him, but he uses a stick to drive us along to the edge of the sea. The townsmen are following, and the stranger, whom Abderus calls Hercules, turns to fight them. He foolishly leaves Abderus in charge of watching us.

While he's gone, we make a feast of Abderus.

Someone must have run back to let our master know what is happening, because he's hurtling down to the beach. We know Diomedes can take on this hero—but after a fierce fight, he is killed.

Hercules lays the body of Diomedes down before us, and we start to feed. Who could have known that this is the cure we all needed? Once we finish consuming our master, our drive to eat human flesh disappears, and we become far more interested in oats and hay.

As Hercules buries his friend, we hear him promise to build the city of Abdera in his honor. Then he binds our mouths—just in case—and herds us back to King Eurystheus.

A Boisterous Battle

Hercules' eighth labor—stealing the man-eating mares of Diomedes—was one of his most dangerous. It sent him all the way to the land of Thrace, not far from the Black Sea. On the way there, however, he managed to fit in yet another death-defying adventure.

Hercules stopped at the house of his friend King Admetus (ad-MEE-tis) to stay for a while. Although his friend welcomed him, offering him food, drink, and rest, it was clear the household was in mourning for someone. Who had died? When Hercules asked, he was told that it was someone not terribly important. Do not worry about it, the family reassured him. But Hercules felt that something was amiss. The staff working in the house seemed far too upset, and they were shocked when they saw him eating, drinking, and enjoying music as if nothing were wrong.

Soon, Hercules found out the truth from one of the servants. The person they mourned was Alkestis (al-KES-tiss), his friend's wife. The god

In this 1871 painting by Frederic Leighton, Hercules battles Thanatos (Death) for the life of Alkestis.

Apollo had promised that Admetus could postpone his fated day of death if he found someone to die in his place. Alkestis chose to die so that her husband could live. In some versions of the tale, she was already gone by the time Hercules arrived. Others state that she was in the process of dying. Euripides wrote in the play *Alcestis*, "Oh yes, he [Admetus] is crying. He holds his wife close in his arms, imploring her not to forsake him. What he wants is impossible. She is dying. The sickness fades her now. She has gone slack, just an inert weight on the arm."[1]

Not sure what else he should do, in some versions, Hercules traveled directly to the Underworld to bring her back. There, he met Thanatos (THAN-uh-tohs), the son of Nyx (Night) and brother of Hypnos (Sleep). Thanatos was the god of nonviolent death. He appeared to those who died, gently took a lock of their hair, and then led them into the Underworld. When Thanatos tried to stop Hercules from taking Alkestis, they wrestled until the young hero won. Alkestis was released and allowed to return to the world of the living. In other stories, Hercules tangled with

Thanatos in Alkestis' bedroom, before she was taken to the Underworld. Euripides wrote this version of Hercules' plans:

> I must save this woman who has died so lately, bring Alkestis back to live in this house and pay Admetos all the kindness that I owe. I must go there (to the funeral) and watch for Thanatos of the black robe, master of dead men, and I think I shall find him drinking the blood of slaughtered beasts beside the grave. Then, if I can break suddenly from my hiding place, catch him, and hold him in the circle of these arms, there is no way he will be able to break my hold on his bruised ribs, until he gives the woman up to me. But if I miss my quarry, if he does not come to the clotted offering, I must go down, I must ask the Maiden and the Master in the sunless homes of those below.[2]

English poet John Milton (1608–1674) included Hercules' rescue in his poem "On His Deceased Wife," calling the hero the son of Jove (the Roman version of Zeus). He wrote:

> Methought I saw my late espousèd Saint
> Brought to me like Alcestis from the grave,
> Whom Jove's great son to her glad husband gave,
> Rescued from death by force, though pale and faint.[3]

By the time Hercules had reached the shore where Diomedes lived, he was rested and ready to take on some of the fiercest monsters in all of mythology. In *Imagines*, Philostratus the Elder described the horses of Diomedes: "their manes are unkempt, they are shaggy down to their hoofs, and in every way they resemble wild beasts; their stalls are tainted with flesh and bones of the men Diomedes used as food for his horses, and the breeder of the mares himself is even more savage of aspect than the mares near whom he had fallen."[4]

According to Euripides, once he had founded the city of Abdera on the shores of Thrace, Hercules headed back to the king as assigned. "Next he mounted on a chariot and tamed with the bit the horses of Diomedes, that greedily champed their bloody food at gory mangers with unbridled jaws, devouring with hideous joy the flesh of men; then crossing the heights of Hebrus that flow with silver, he still toiled on for the tyrant of Mycenae."[5]

Of course, the king had no idea what to do with the horses once he had them. One story says that he dedicated the horses to Hera, who bred them and started the line that eventually produced the horses of Alexander the Great. Another story says he allowed them to roam freely for the rest of their lives. A third version states that Hercules had them taken to Olympus as a sacrifice to Zeus. The powerful god did not want them, so he had them eaten by hungry wolves, lions, and bears.

After his next task, which was to obtain the belt of Hippolyte (hih-PAH-lih-tuh), queen of the Amazons, Hercules had succeeded in nine of his twelve labors. The ones he had left would prove to be some of his most difficult. It was time to face the multi-headed monsters Geryon and Cerberus. Both of them would test the hero's strength and courage.

The ruins at Abdera still exist, long after Hercules supposedly founded the city near Thrace.

The Mysterious Minotaur

The Minotaur, the offspring of a woman and a bull, had the head and the tail of a bull but the body of a man. It was a savage animal that caused great fear and destruction on Crete, the island where it lived. King Minos did not know how to control the creature, so he called on his friend and architect Daedalus (DEH-duh-lus) for help. He asked him to build a huge, complicated labyrinth from which absolutely nothing could escape. The Minotaur was placed in it.

Each year, fourteen young Athenians were put inside the labyrinth so that the monster would have something to chase, play with, and then devour. This went on for years until the Greek hero Theseus found out what was going on in the maze and thought it should be stopped. He went to Crete and offered to be one of the people sacrificed to the creature.

The Minotaur

Before he was put into the maze, he fell in love with Minos's daughter, Ariadne (ayr-ee-AD-nee). In return for a promise of marriage, she told him the secret for escaping the labyrinth. As he ventured through the halls, he should unwind a ball of thread behind him so that he could follow it back out. When he came to the Minotaur, Theseus killed it and then, following the thread, led the others to safety.

Theseus also played a role in the fate of the Cretan bull. After Hercules released the animal, it roamed the plains of Marathon, killing livestock and people. Before he left to deal with the Minotaur, Theseus subdued the bull and brought it home to Athens, where he sacrificed it to Apollo. Later in life, Theseus became the king of Athens.

Going up against a monster with as many bodies and limbs as Geryon was scary—but Hercules, armed with his special bow and arrows, managed to strike him down.

MONSTERS OF HERCULES

CHAPTER 5

The Curse of Too Many Heads

"Geryon! Come quick!" My neighbor Menoetes (meh-noh-EE-teez) crashes through my door, screeching about a powerful man who is trying to steal my cattle. Orthus, my two-headed hound and the brother of Cerberus, had attacked the stranger. With teeth flashing, the dog fought to protect the cattle but was struck down by the man's mighty club. Next, I was told, my herder Eurytion (yur-IH-tee-on), a centaur, rushed at the man and was also killed. How could this be?

My pride and joy is my precious herd of cattle. To keep them safe from thieves, I live at the end of the world, near the setting sun, and kept Orthus and Eurytion to watch over the herds.

As I tremble with rage, my mother, Callirrhoe (kah-LIH-roh-ee), an Oceanid and daughter of two Titans, tries to calm me. I have three sets of legs, six arms, and three heads—and am a formidable fighter. "What harm can come to me, Mother?" I cry. "My father was Poseidon's son Chrysaor [KRIH-say-or], who sprang from the blood of Medusa as Perseus beheaded her. Am I not immortal? If I am, this stranger cannot harm me. But if he can, I'd rather die than let some thief make off with my cattle!"

As I stomp to the pasture to protect my property, I am amazed by the size and apparent strength of this golden-haired stranger—but I know I can take him on. He throws a stone, which knocks a helmet off one of my heads. I roar and grab him, and the man clubs another head. The pain makes me release him, and he skitters backward out of my grasp. He draws his bow and I laugh. A simple arrow is not enough to stop me—but when it finds purchase in my chest, I realize it has been coated in the poison of the Hydra. As I collapse to the ground, I mourn the loss of my precious cattle. What will happen to them?

Capturing the Cattle

To complete his tenth mission, Hercules had to travel west to the island of Erythea, near modern-day Spain. Because this is where they saw the sun set, the Greeks believed it was the end of the world. Hercules had to borrow the goblet of the sun god, Helios, in order to sail that far. On his way, say some of the tales, he was blocked by a series of cliffs. Hercules forced them apart, forming two huge mountains—one in Europe and the other in Africa. They became known as the Pillars of Hercules. The strait of water between these mountains (the Strait of Gibraltar) connects the Mediterranean Sea to the Atlantic Ocean.

Once Hercules had the herd of cattle, he had to get them back to King Eurystheus. He used Helios's goblet for part of the journey, but once he returned it to the sun god, he had to go on foot. Hercules had as many adventures coming back with the herd as he did on the way there. It seemed as if everyone wanted to steal the animals, including Cacus, the fire-breathing, man-eating son of Vulcan, the Roman god of fire. When Hercules went after him, Cacus, afraid for the first time in his life, blocked the door to his cave with a boulder. Hercules simply took the top off the mountain and rained stones and tree limbs onto him. When Cacus wouldn't give up, Hercules leaped into the cave and strangled him.

Meanwhile, Hera was still trying to complicate his life as much as possible. When Hercules was back on the road, she sent a gadfly to torment the cattle. It made them scatter throughout the region of Thrace. He

Hercules and Cacus, a marble sculpture in Rome, was carved by Baccio Bandinelli of Florence from 1525 to 1534.

was eventually able to gather most of them together again, but the ones he lost became wild.

The Last of the Labors

Hercules' next to last mission also took him to the far ends of the earth. He had to retrieve the golden apples of the garden of the Hesperides (hes-PAYR-ih-deez). The apples—a wedding gift to Zeus and Hera—were guarded by a serpent called Ladon (whom Apollodorus gave one hundred heads.[1]) In most tales, this monster is slain by other men, but in some, Hercules faces the dragon and kills it with his poisoned arrows. In *Argonautica*, Apollonius writes about how the Argonauts, men who traveled with the hero Jason, came to the garden and found the monster dead:

> The snake lay fallen by the trunk of the apple tree. Only the tip of his tail was still twitching, but from his head to the end of his dark spine he lay lifeless. Where the arrows had left in his blood the sharp venom of the Lernaean Hydra, flies wilted and died on the festering wounds. Nearby, the Hesperides made shrill lament. . . .[2]

Having traveled to the ends of the earth, Hercules would finally have to face the Underworld—where few had ever gone and come back.

Into the Underworld

What happened before I faced the golden-haired fool was somewhat of a mystery to me. Someone told me that he went before the god Hades (HAY-deez) and his queen, Persephone (per-SEH-fuh-nee). Clearly, this was a brave—or stupid—man. Rumor has it that when asked why he had traveled to their realm of the dead, this man explained he was on a last mission. Hades was angry—because the stranger accidentally pricked him with a poison-tipped arrow, and Hades had to be healed on Olympus—but Persephone took pity on the man.

What was his mission? Capturing me of all things! Me—the guard of the gates of the Underworld! Me—the child of Echidna and Typhon. I wasn't too worried, though. Hades said he could take me to King

Eurystheus only if he could capture me without using any weapons, and he had to return me to the Underworld once he had proven to Eurystheus that he had conquered me.

When the so-called hero found me, the fight was on. It was a long and difficult battle for both of us. My tail, made of serpents, lashed out again and again. How angry it made me that he was protected from the venomous bites by the lion's skin he wore. Nothing could penetrate it, not even the fangs of the snakes that made up my tail. When I spun my heads back around to face him, this man reached around my necks and began to squeeze. How could a simple man be this strong? I fought. I struggled. I gasped for air. Finally, I had no choice but to give up fighting.

Oh the embarrassment. He threw me over his shoulder and carried me all the way back to King Eurystheus. When the king realized that this man had been able to capture even me, he hid in fear. I certainly can't blame him. Having proven himself, Hercules returned me to the Underworld as promised. At least he kept his word.

A man of his word, Hercules allowed Cerberus to return to the Underworld after he proved he could capture him in the first place.

The Most Dangerous Mission of All

As brave as Hercules was, he knew that his last mission would be the riskiest, as Cerberus was one of the scariest monsters of all. In Hesiod's *Theogony*, the author describes the dog's chore in the Underworld by writing, "Wagging his tail and drooping his ears he fawns on those who enter, though he never lets them go back out again, but lies in wait and devours anyone he catches trying to pass out of the gates."[3]

Most likely, King Eurystheus saved this one for last because he was so sure that no one, not even Hercules, could survive the job.

How many heads Cerberus actually had depends on which story you read or which drawing you see. A great deal of art shows him with one or two heads or sometimes three. Hesiod, on the other hand, describes the creature as "A monster not to be overcome and that may not be described, Cerberus who eats raw flash, the brazen-voiced hound of Hades, fifty-headed, relentless and strong."[4] Others have said that the creature was a mix of dog and dragon with serpents for a tail and a mane down his back. His mother was Echidna; his father was Typhon, making the dog a sibling of the Hydra and of Orthus. Cerberus was so powerful, in fact, that even the gods of Olympus trembled at the thought of confronting him.

Hercules understandably took some precautions before he left. He went to Eleusis to see a priest named Eumolpus (yoo-MUL-pus) to find out some of the secret religious ceremonies that helped protect a person in the Underworld. Next, he went to Taenarum, a place where heroes could slip into the afterlife without having to die first. Hermes, the messenger god, would accompany him.

In the Underworld, Hercules wandered among the souls of the dead. Most of them scattered as far from him as possible, overwhelmed by such a hero in their midst. While he was there he met a dead hero named Meleager (meh-lee-AY-gur). Hercules was so impressed with the man, he asked if he could marry his sister. Meleager agreed to let him marry Deianeira (day-uh-NAYR-uh).

Next, Hercules encountered two other heroes, Theseus and Peirithous. They had snuck into the Underworld to take Persephone back to earth, but had been caught. Hercules was able to free Theseus, but the ground shook when he tried to rescue Peirithous, so he had to leave him.

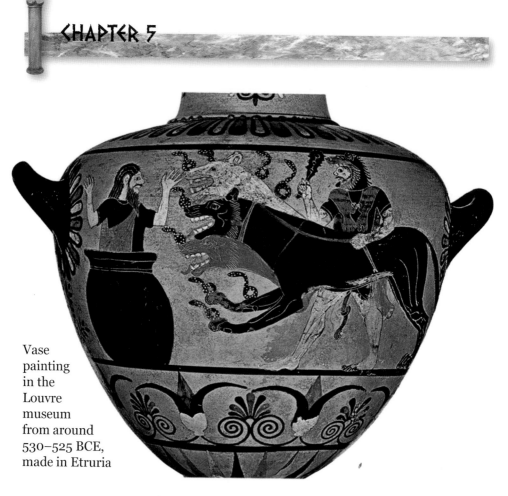

Vase painting in the Louvre museum from around 530–525 BCE, made in Etruria

Not Quite the End

At last, his long years of labor were over. His sins were forgiven and his soul wiped clean of the horrors that Hera's jealousy had forced upon him. Not only had he conquered some of the fiercest and most dangerous monsters in the world, he was known throughout Greek society as the bravest and most beloved of heroes.

Hercules' adventures did not end there. In later years, he helped rescue a maiden from a hungry sea monster and even fought alongside Zeus to defeat the Giants before they could take control of Mount Olympus. He rescued Prometheus from an eagle that was preying on him for eternity. And as he promised while he was in the Underworld, he married Deianeira. Indirectly, she led to his death. She gave him a cloak as a gift to ensure that he loved her more than any other maiden. However, unbeknownst to her, the cloak was poisoned. When Hercules put it on, he was in great pain. Some stories say that he had a funeral pyre built on Mount Olympus and he threw himself on it. Instead of waiting for death to come to him, he went to death instead. Other stories say that the gods took pity on his pain, and Athena arranged for him to be brought to Mount Olympus and live forever with the gods as they had intended for him long, long ago.

The Role of Hercules and His Monsters

Of all the many figures within Greek and Roman mythology, none of them represented the beauty, strength, and power of youth the way Hercules did. He was a hero among heroes—a foe that could not be beaten by any monster, let alone a mere human.

The young man was challenged by the gods, and for many, he was almost like a god. He faced the biggest monsters known—often with nothing more than his bare hands. He never gave up or gave in. He did some things that were not exactly honorable, but in stories about heroes, these downfalls were accepted as part of their humanity.

Children told each other stories of Hercules' feats with awe, inspiring one another to be braver or tougher. Parents told these stories to their children to show them the results of determination and courage. Young women whispered stories of this blond, muscled man to each other with giggles and blushes. Young men thought about the stories to understand what it took to become a hero. Some boasted to be descendents of the mighty hero to make themselves look more important.

Over the years, countless pieces of art have been dedicated to mythology's favorite hero. Besides ancient urns, he is found in statues, painting, sculptures, and other art. He was worshiped in temples.

The monsters he fought played an important role as well—after all, without monsters to defeat, a hero could not prove his mettle. Many of the monsters Hercules faced were immortalized as constellations: Leo the Lion; Hydra the Water Serpent; Cancer the Crab; and Canis Major, the Greater Dog. These shapes may have been inspired by the stories told about the monsters—or the other way around. Even Hercules himself was immortalized in a constellation—the fifth largest one. He stands with his club raised over Draco, who represents Ladon, the serpent from the Garden of the Hesperides.

Welcome to the Underworld

According to Greek mythology, the Underworld was the kingdom of the dead. It is where all human souls went to spend the afterlife. It was ruled over by Hades, and in many stories, it was home to supernatural beings such as fairies, demons, and giants. It was surrounded by a number of rivers. The Acheron was the river of woe. The Cocytus was the river of lamentation. The Phlegethon was the river of fire, and the Lethe was the river of forgetfulness. The other river was Styx,

The journey across the water of the Underworld was a slow and profound one, giving the rider the chance to reflect on the life he or she had lived.

the river that gave immortality, and by which the gods would swear unbreakable oaths.

There were only two possible ways to get into the Underworld. The first one was to die. The second way was to travel through special underground caves. Once in the Underworld, the first challenge was to get across the Styx. The newly dead waited on its shore for transport across in a ferryboat piloted by Charon (KAYR-on). To get a ride, the dead had to pay Charon a coin—and they had to be dead. Families made sure that when a loved one died, they placed a coin for Charon on his or her body. Without the coin, they wandered on the shore of the river for eternity.

The dead lived in a state of forgetfulness in the Underworld. If they committed heinous crimes while alive, they were kept in an Underworld chamber called Tartarus. If they were heroes, they stayed in the Elysian Fields, where they could converse with one another, play games, and enjoy the food that grew in the perfect weather of the fields.

Chapter 1. A Moment of Madness

1. Homer, *The Odyssey*, translated by E. V. Rieu (New York: Penguin Classics, 2010), Book 11, lines 620–623.
2. Homer, *The Iliad*, translated by Robert Fagles, (New York: Penguin Classics, 2003), Book 19, lines 124–133.

Chapter 2. A Powerful Mane, an Immortal Head

1. Euripides, *Heracles*, translated by E. P. Coleridge, Internet Classics Archive, line 359, http://classics.mit.edu/Euripides/heracles.html

Chapter 3. From a Boar to the Birds

1. Pausanias, *Description of Greece*, translated by W.H.S. Jones (online text version), 8.22.5, http://www.theoi.com/Text/Pausanias8B.html
2. Homer, *The Iliad*, translated by Robert Fagles, (New York: Penguin Classics, 2003), Book 23, lines 361–367.

Chapter 4. Capturing a Bull, Catching a Herd

1. Euripides, *Alcestis* (online text version), lines 201 ff., http://www.theoi.com/Daimon/Thanatos.html
2. Ibid., 839 ff.
3. Thomas Bulfinch, *Bulfinch's Mythology: Age of Fable, Stories of Gods and Heroes* (online text version), http://classiclit.about.com/library/bl-etexts/tbulfinch/bl-tbulfinch-age-23.htm

4. Philostratus the Elder, *Imagines*, translated by Arthur Fairbanks (online text version), 2.25, http://www.theoi.com/Text/PhilostratusElder1A.html
5. Euripides, *Heracles*, translated by E.P. Coleridge, Internet Classics Archive, lines 380–385, http://classics.mit.edu/Euripides/heracles.html

Chapter 5. The Curse of Too Many Heads

1. Apollodorus, *The Library*, translated by J. G. Frazer, Loeb Classical Library Volumes 121 & 122 (Cambridge, MA: Harvard University Press; London: William Heinemann Ltd., 1921), 2.5.11, http://www.theoi.com/Text/Apollodorus1.html
2. Apollonius, *Argonautica*, translated by R. C. Seaton, Internet Classics Archive, 4.1383–1449, http://classics.mit.edu/Apollonius/argon.4.iv.html
3. Hesiod, *Theogony* (online text version), 770–773; translated by Hugh G. Evelyn-White, http://www.perseus.tufts.edu/hopper/text?doc=Perseus:abo:tlg,0020,001:769
4. Ibid., 310.

MONSTERS OF HERCULES

FURTHER READING

For Young Adults

Denton, Shannon Eric. *Hercules Short Tales*. Edina, Minnesota: Magic Wagon, 2008.

Huber, Michal. *Mythematics: Solving the Twelve Labors of Hercules*. Princeton, New Jersey: Princeton University Press, 2009.

Limke, Jeff. *Theseus: Battling the Minotaur*. Minneapolis, Minnesota: Graphic Universe, 2008.

McCaughrean, Geraldine, *Hercules*. Peterborough, New Hampshire: Cricket Books, 2005.

Saunders, Nick. *The Twelve Labors of Hercules*. Milwaukee, Wisconsin: World Almanac Library, 2007.

Storrie, Paul. *Hercules: The Twelve Labors*. Minneapolis, Minnesota: Graphic Universe, 2007.

Works Consulted

Apollodorus. *The Library*. Translated by Sir James George Frazer. Cambridge, MA: Harvard University Press; London: William Heinemann Ltd., 1921. http://www.theoi.com/Text/Apollodorus1.html

Apollonius. *Argonautica*. Translated by R. C. Seaton. Internet Classics Archive. http://classics.mit.edu/Apollonius/argon.4.iv.html

Bulfinch, Thomas. *Myths of Greece and Rome*. New York: Penguin Books, 1979.

Cotterell, Arthur. *Classical Mythology*. New York: Lorenz Books, 2000.

Euripides. *Alcestis*. Translated by Richard Aldington. Internet Classics Archive. http://classics.mit.edu/Euripides/alcestis.html

———. *Heracles*. Translated by E. P. Coleridge. Internet Classics Archive. http://classics.mit.edu/Euripides/heracles.html

Hamilton, Edith. *Mythology*. New York: Grand Central Publishing, 1942.

Hesiod. *The Homeric Hymns and Homerica*. English Translation by Hugh G. Evelyn-White. Cambridge, MA: Harvard University Press; London: William Heinemann Ltd., 1914.

———. *The Theogony of Hesiod*. Translated by Hugh G. Evelyn-White. 1914. http://www.sacred-texts.com/cla/hesiod/theogony.htm

Homer. *The Odyssey*. New York: Penguin Classics, 2010.

Homer. *The Iliad*. New York: Penguin Classics, 2003.

March, Jenny. *Cassell's Dictionary of Classical Mythology*. London: Cassell & Co., 2001.

———. *The Penguin Book of Classical Myths*. New York: Penguin Books, 2008.

Pausanias. *Description of Greece*. Translated by W.H.S. Jones. Classical E-Text. http://www.theoi.com/Text/Pausanias8B.html

Philostratus the Elder. *Imagines*. Translated by Arthur Fairbanks. Classical E-Text. http://www.theoi.com/Text/PhilostratusElder1A.html

FURTHER READING

On the Internet
Herakles—for History and Science Middle School Kids
http://www.historyforkids.org/learn/greeks/religion/myths/herakles.htm
Hercules/Heracles
http://greece.mrdonn.org/greekgods/hercules.html
Hercules/Mythology for Kids/12 Labors
http://people.uncw.edu/deagona/herakles/children/home.html
The Labors of Hercules from Greek Mythology
http://www.mythweb.com/hercules/
The Twelve Labors of Hercules
http://www.factmonster.com/ipka/A0882073.html

GLOSSARY

castanets (kas-teh-NETS)—Hand-held musical instruments, usually made of shells, wood, or metal, that make a loud noise when banged together.

catapult (KAT-uh-pult)—A military device for launching stones, arrows, or other missiles.

constellation (kon-stuh-LAY-shun)—A group of stars that appear to make a picture in the sky.

exile (EK-zyl)—To be separated from one's homeland.

gadfly (GAD-fly)—A type of fly that bites domestic animals.

goblet—A bowl-shaped vessel for holding liquids.

immortality (ih-mor-TAL-ih-tee)—The ability to live forever.

labyrinth (LAB-rinth)—A complex maze, often underground.

lyre (LYR)—A stringed musical instrument of ancient Greece.

mortal (MOR-tul)—A human; a being with a definite lifespan.

mosaic (moh-ZAY-ik)—Artwork that is typically made from many small pieces of colored tile.

nymph (NIMF)—Any of the minor nature deities that lived in the mountains, streams, trees, or other natural settings.

Oceanid (oh-shee-AN-id)—Any of the three thousand daughters of Oceanus; nymphs who lived in the ocean.

oracle (OR-uh-kul)—A priest or priestess that gives predictions or advice; the ancient Greeks believed oracles spoke for a god.

precaution (pre-KAW-shun)—A measure taken in advance to avoid possible evil or danger.

pyre (PYR)—A pile or heap of wood for burning a dead body as part of the funeral rites.

strait (STRAYT)—A narrow passage of water connecting two larger bodies of water.

INDEX